Diary of a

Pilot

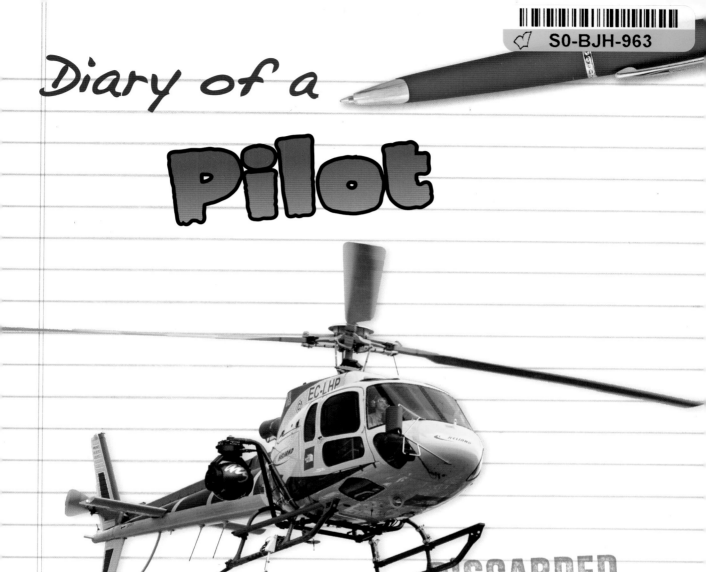

Angela Royston

Heinemann
LIBRARY
Chicago, Illinois

© 2014 Heinemann Library
an imprint of Capstone Global Library, LLC
Chicago, Illinois

To contact Capstone Global Library, please call 800-747-4992,
or visit our web site www.capstonepub.com

Edited by Daniel Nunn, Rebecca Rissman, and Catherine Veitch
Designed by Cynthia Akiyoshi
Picture research by Ruth Blair
Production by Victoria Fitzgerald
Originated by Capstone Global Library Ltd
Printed and bound in China by South China Printing Company Ltd

17 16 15 14 13
10 9 8 7 6 5 4 3 2 1

Library of Congress Cataloging-in-Publication Data
Royston, Angela, 1945-
  Pilot / Angela Royston.
    pages cm.(Diary of a...)
  Includes bibliographical references and index.
  ISBN 978-1-4329-7584-5 (hb)—ISBN 978-1-4329-7591-3 (pb)
  1. Helicopters—Piloting—Juvenile literature. 2. Helicopter pilots—
Juvenile literature. I. Title.
  TL716.5.R69 2014
  629.132'5252—dc23
                                    2012046862

Acknowledgments
We would like to thank the following for permission to reproduce
photographs: Corbis pp. 4 (© Construction Photography), 11
(© Charles E. Rotkin), 14 (© Saed Hindash/Star Ledger), 21 (©
doc-stock), 27 (© John Nakata); Getty Images pp. 6, 7 (Chris
Ratcliffe/Bloomberg), 8 (Bernhard Limberger), 10, 22 (Alberto
Incrocci), 12 (Julian Love), 17 (German Garcia/AFP), 19 (Arnulf
Husmo), 20 (Jeff J Mitchell), 23 (Tyler J. Clements/U.S. Navy);
Shutterstock pp. title page (© Natursports), contents page (©
Leo Francini), 5 (© Ivan Cholakov), 15 (© James A. Harris), 18
(© Zastol`skiy Victor Leonidovich), 24 (© bikeriderlondon), 25
(© bajars), 28 diary (© Pavel Vakhrushev), 28 pen (© Phant);
Superstock pp. 9, 26 (imagebroker.net), 13 (Justin Guariglia /
age fotostock), 16 (Transtock).

Background and design features reproduced with permission of
Shutterstock. Cover photograph of helicopter pilot reproduced
with permission of Corbis (© Chris Crisman).

We would like to thank Olivia Milles for her invaluable help in the
preparation of this book.

Every effort has been made to contact copyright holders of
material reproduced in this book. Any omissions will be rectified
in subsequent printings if notice is given to the publisher.

Some words are shown in bold, **like this**. You can find
out what they mean by looking in the Glossary.

Contents

One of the Lucky Ones

I am a helicopter pilot. I work for a company that flies workers to **oil rigs** out at sea. I'm lucky to have this job. There aren't many jobs for helicopter pilots.

oil rig

It is important to do safety checks while the helicopter is still on the ground.

Flying a helicopter takes skill. These aircraft have just one main engine. If the engine failed, I would have to make an emergency landing on the water! This is my diary for one week.

Taking Off

Sunday, May 12

This morning, I flew to an **oil rig**. Before I set off, I checked that the helicopter was filled with fuel and was ready for takeoff. Then I started the engine and the **rotors** turned above me.

rotors

engine

My passengers were workers employed on the oil rig, so they knew the journey well. When the **air traffic controller** gave us the **all clear**, we lifted off.

The Flight

The oil company insists that we leave and arrive on time. I flew at a safe height above the sea. There was a bit of wind, but not too much.

I kept a close eye on the flight instruments in the **cockpit** and reached the **oil rig** an hour later. I've flown there many times, so I knew exactly where to land.

Landing on the Rig

When we reached the **oil rig**, another helicopter was just about to take off. I waited and then landed. The oil workers climbed out and got ready to start work.

Half an hour on an oil rig is enough for me, but the men work here for a week or longer. My return passengers were workers who were starting a week-long break. They were eager to get going!

A Round Trip

Monday, May 13

Today I had Mick, a new pilot, with me. I showed him the three **oil rigs** we were flying to on the map. He typed the route into the **navigation system**.

navigation system

Mick was an experienced pilot, but flying to oil rigs was new to him. I showed him the best approach for landing on each rig. Then he flew the helicopter back to **base**.

Training

Mick told me about his training. He went to flying school and got a license to fly **fixed-wing planes**. Then he trained to fly helicopters. It all cost him a lot of money.

fixed-wing plane

I did it differently. I joined the army, which paid for my training. I flew helicopters that carried supplies from one **base** to another. On one flight, I had a heavy truck dangling below the helicopter!

Exciting Past

Tuesday, May 14

Mick asked me what other jobs I'd done, so I told him about the years I spent flying police helicopters. It was fun to find and track **suspects** from the air!

I also told him how I spent one summer fighting **wildfires**. It was exciting, but dangerous. We flew low over the sea and scooped up water to dump on the flames.

Rough Seas

Wednesday, May 15

We had our own excitement today. There was a strong wind—too strong for our normal flights—but we had a call from one of the **oil rigs** that someone had hurt himself.

I took a doctor with us, but he didn't look too happy when we reached the rig. The wind was blowing so hard that I wasn't sure I could land safely.

Emergency Airlift

I hovered over the landing pad while the doctor was lowered from a **rescue hoist**. Luckily, the wind died down for a few minutes, so I could land the helicopter on the **oil rig**.

rescue hoist

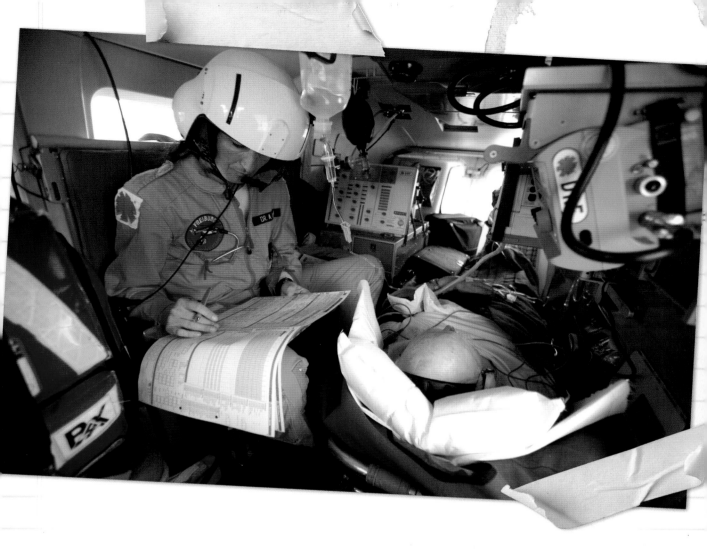

The worker's leg was badly broken. The doctor patched him up and then we lifted him into the helicopter. I set off and flew the injured man straight to the landing site at the hospital.

Another Problem!

Thursday, May 16

I was more than halfway toward an **oil rig** today when the **tail rotors** started acting up. I made it to the rig, but I couldn't solve the problem. I called the main office.

They said there was a helicopter mechanic on the rig who could fix it. That was lucky! He managed to fix the problem. I hope nothing else goes wrong!

Carrying Bosses

Friday, May 17

Today, I flew three of the company directors from the main office to one of the **oil rigs**. They asked me to wait until their meeting was over.

Then I flew them from the rig to one of the
company offices in another city. We landed
on the roof, then stayed overnight in a hotel.
The food in the restaurant was great!

What Next?

Saturday, May 18

The next day, I flew back to the main office alone. I thought about what job I'd like to do next. The company has an **air rescue** branch, so maybe I could do that?

Helicopters can rescue people from places that are very hard to get to.

Cameramen can get great shots from a helicopter.

I would also like to work for a television company, flying to disaster areas and big events. But everyone wants that job, and those who have it never leave!

Writing a Diary

A pilot writes a log of everything that happens. The log records facts such as the time the helicopter took off, what the weather was like, and the time it landed. This book, however, is a diary. It tells what happened from the pilot's point of view.

You can write a diary, too! Your diary can describe your life—what you saw, what you felt, and the events that happened.

Here are some tips for writing a diary:

- Start each entry with the day and the date. You don't have to include an entry for every day.

- The entries should be in **chronological** order, which means that they follow the order in which events happened.

- Use the past tense when you are writing about something that has already happened.

- Remember that a diary is the writer's story, so use "I" and "my."

Glossary

air rescue when a helicopter crew rescues people who are in danger at sea

air traffic controller person at an airport who tells pilots when they can take off and land

all clear message or signal that tells a pilot that it is safe to take off or land

base headquarters

chronological in order of time

cockpit place in the front of an aircraft where the pilot sits to fly the helicopter or airplane

fixed-wing plane airplane with wings that do not move

navigation system method of finding the way

oil rig metal structure that supports a huge drill. The drill digs through the rocks to reach oil that lies deep below the ground. Some oil rigs are out in the middle of the sea.

rescue hoist machine that winds in a thick wire or rope. On a helicopter, a rescue hoist is used to lift someone on or off the helicopter while it is in the air.

rotor blade that spins in a circle above a helicopter to lift it off the ground

suspect person who the police think may have committed a crime

tail rotor smaller blade at the back of the helicopter that stops the main rotors from making the helicopter spin

wildfire large fire that spreads quickly and destroys large areas

Find Out More

Books

Bodden, Valerie. *Helicopters* (Rescue Vehicles). Mankato, Minn.: Creative Education, 2011.

Colson, Rob. *Helicopters* (Ultimate Machines). New York: PowerKids, 2013.

Langley, Andrew. *Helicopters* (Machines on the Move). Mankato, Minn.: Amicus, 2011.

Internet sites

Facthound offers a safe, fun way to find Internet sites related to this book. All of the sites on Facthound have been researched by our staff.

Here's all you do:
Visit www.facthound.com
Type in this code: 9781432975845

Index